I'D RATHER EAT FROM THE KING'S TABLE

A Spiritual & Natural Healing Journey

Angela R. Fleming

Creative Touch Publishing LLC.

P.O. Box 7482
Warner Robins, GA 31095

Printed and bound in the
United States of America

BOOK COVER ILLUSTRATION by
India S. Fleming

1. Spiritual. 2. Motivational. 3. Non-Fiction.

International Standard Book Number
979-8-234-06441-7

TABLE OF CONTENTS

DEDICATION

First, I want to honor and dedicate this book back to my Lord and Savior, Jesus Christ.

I also dedicate this book to my husband, Marquis, and my daughters, Isis and India. Thank you for your unwavering encouragement, for faithfully covering me in prayer, and for your constant support through every challenging moment of my healing journey. I am deeply grateful for the sacrifices you made.

Finally, I dedicate this book to my parents, William H. and Annie E. Smith. My father lived each day in faithful devotion to the Lord and humbly sought God on his knees. He remained steadfast in prayer until the Lord blessed and graciously delivered him from his own affliction, prior to his passing. My mother is a faithful woman of God who continually pursues the heart of Jesus. She serves others selflessly and is always willing to help others, as the Lord leads her.

ACKNOWLEDGEMENTS

I would like to acknowledge my Overseers, Apostle Daniel L. Akins and Pastor Vonyett Akins; Pastor Nana Yaa Henaku Larbi; and the leadership team at More Sure Word Church in Warner Robins, Georgia, for faithfully laboring in prayer on my behalf throughout my healing process.

I also want to extend a special thanks to Prophet Kevin Powe, founder of Destroy the Destroyer Ministries in Trenton, New Jersey. I was first introduced to his ministry online, between 2023 and 2024. His teachings on consecration and the necessity of dying to the flesh deeply resonated with my spirit. Although I desired to be used by God, I came to the realize this was the missing piece in my personal walk with God. Prophet Powe's message on living a consecrated life helped me understand that God can truly use me when I surrender myself to Him daily. Thank you, Prophet Kevin Powe, for your transformative teachings on what it means to live a life fully consecrated to God.

INTRODUCTION

“I’d Rather Eat from the King’s Table" is more than a title. . . it is my personal testimony of how God’s divine provision and His unchanging Word became the source of my survival, my deep internal healing, and ultimately, my life as a walking miracle.

I have come to understand that God’s Word is a living seed. Just as physical food provides the nutrients our bodies need to function, God’s Truth provides the essential nourishment our souls require to thrive. There is a profound connection between the spiritual and the natural. When we choose to honor our bodies as the temple of the Holy Spirit and turn away from what is "unclean," both in what we consume and in what we believe, we align ourselves with the rhythm of Heaven.

By choosing the King's portions over the offerings of the world, we position ourselves to receive the supernatural healing designed for our bodies and our minds. This journey is about far more than physical health; it is about the transformative power of divine alignment.

Join me on this journey as we explore the supernatural healing power found only at the King's table.

THE DAY OF MY AFFLICTION

On May 25, 2023, my body was suddenly afflicted. I began falling repeatedly, vomiting, and losing control of my bladder. Similar incidents occurred in 2020, particularly during exercise and while repeatedly climbing stairs as I helped move my children into college. During that time, I visited the doctor and underwent several tests, including an MRI. Despite these evaluations, no clear diagnosis was identified, and I was simply prescribed steroids for inflammation.

The next time I went walking the Lord instructed me to pray beforehand, which I did. However, I added push-ups on a park bench to my routine; something that was not part of God's instruction to me and was, instead, an act of disobedience.

Within a few days, I experienced a sudden, sharp pain in my left arm, as if it were being violently pulled from its socket. My husband urged me to go to the emergency room, but I resisted, believing the pain would subside. When it did not, I asked him to take me to a chiropractor, assuming the pain was caused by a pinched nerve, as I had also been experiencing discomfort in my neck and shoulder while sleeping. I thought an adjustment to my neck and shoulder would relieve the pain in my arm. It was then that I clearly heard the Holy Spirit say, *"That chiropractor isn't a doctor. You need to see a doctor."*

Once again, I disobeyed God, and went to the chiropractor to get an adjustment. After adjusting my neck and shoulder, the chiropractor explained that it would take some time for the pain to fully subside. For a few days, the discomfort slightly eased. Then, one morning I woke up unable to move my left arm.

At that point, I agreed to visit the Med Stop to find out what was happening. My daughter drove me, as I was unable to do so myself. Upon examining me, the medical staff was unable to identify the cause of my condition. The on-duty physician prescribed steroids to address the pain and inflammation, but the medication provided no relief and I continued to experience severe pain.

As my condition worsened and became unbearable, my husband took me to Houston Medical Center for further evaluation. The attending nurse ordered both an MRI and a CT scan. After hours of waiting, the doctor finally returned with the results. He walked into the room and abruptly stated that I had Multiple Sclerosis (MS), then turned and walked away without offering any explanation to me or my husband.

According to the Mayo Clinic, Multiple Sclerosis is a disease that damages the protective covering of nerves. It can cause symptoms such as numbness, weakness, difficulty walking, vision changes, and other neurological impairments.

Shortly thereafter, an ER nurse entered the room with my discharge papers and informed me that I would need to seek further care at the Multiple Sclerosis Institute in Atlanta. I was also informed that I would need to undergo three days of steroid therapy. I informed the nurse that steroids had not been effective for me in the past and she explained that the medication prescribed at Med Stop was a low dosage. She further explained that the therapy they were prescribing me would be significantly stronger.

I called my daughter and instructed her to contact our pastor with the news. Our pastor responded firmly, saying, *"No, your mother does not have MS."*

While waiting to begin therapy and for an appointment call from the Atlanta Multiple Sclerosis Institute, I informed the leaders of my local church of what was happening and asked them to pray for me. As Scripture says in James 5:14, **"Is any sick among you? let him call for the elders of the church..." (KJV).** *I* also informed my mother and my siblings and asked them to pray. I also instructed them not to share the information with anyone else because I was determined to overcome and beat this.

During that time, I committed myself to prayer and to reading the Bible. One night, God came to me in a dream and gave me clear instructions not to look at or entertain anything negative. At the time, I did not fully understand why, but then Proverbs 23:7 came to mind, **"For as he thinketh in his heart, so is he" (KJV).** It was then that I came to understand... the Lord did not want me to be surrounded by or influenced by anything negative or not of Him. He didn't want negativity to take root in my mind nor in my heart. I had to guard both.

Isaiah 26:3 declares, **"Thou wilt keep him in perfect peace, whose mind is stayed on thee: because he trusteth in thee" (KJV).**

That morning, I got up and sent a message to my family and in-laws, telling them not to visit or call, while reassuring them that I was okay. I knew that if I allowed them to, they would be overwhelmed by the condition I was in, and their concerns would only distract me from focusing on my healing process, as I needed to. I turned off every television in the house and intentionally entered the presence of the Lord through prayer and the reading of His Word. I needed to separate myself from the noise and focus solely on God. As Scripture says in 2 Corinthians 6:17, **"Wherefore come out from among**

them, and be ye separate, saith the Lord" (KJV).

I asked God to forgive me for all my sins, and my husband and I made the decision to seek additional medical opinions. Of the two doctors we consulted with, only one took the time to explain the hospital test results. She explained that the scans revealed white spots on my brain and noted that, while they could indicate lupus, she believed multiple sclerosis (MS) was more likely. She also shared that medication could help me live a normal life.

After returning home, I began the three-day course of steroid therapy as prescribed. However, after completing the final treatment, I still experienced no relief, and the pain in my left arm remained intense. As I sat at my kitchen table, exhausted and hurting, God spoke clearly to me, saying, *"I am the Balm of Gilead."*

Jeremiah 8:22 asks, **"Is there no balm in Gilead? Is there no physician there? Why then has the (spiritual) health of the daughter of my people not been restored" (AMP)?**

In that moment, I knew without a doubt that God is my Healer. As I studied the meaning of the Balm of Gilead, I came to understand that it was twofold: God was healing me both spiritually and physically. I recognized that He was addressing not only my relationship with Him, but also the food I was consuming.

I shared what the Lord had revealed to me with my husband, and together we began researching fruit and vegetables known to help improve and overcome the symptoms that showed up as MS. We also searched out testimonies of others who had overcome the symptoms associated with MS. Proverbs 25:2 says, **"It is the glory of God to conceal a thing: but the honor of kings is to search out a matter" (KJV)**. Through research, we discovered that the inflammation in my body was a key component of Multiple Sclerosis that is caused by processed foods.

Everyone in my household decided to stop eating fast food and processed foods, including those from the freezer section in grocery stores; although at that time, we continued eating out at restaurants. I also began taking supplements to support my brain health and reduce the inflammation in my body.

A few days later, while walking into the bathroom, I experienced a sharp pain in my left leg that caused me to fall. I tried to catch myself, but I realized I couldn't move my left arm. I fell onto the bathroom floor.

Because I was home alone, I had to slide across the floor using the right side of my body to enter the bedroom so I could get my phone and call for help. I asked God to give me the strength to get across the room, and He did just that.

My husband rushed home to help me up, but he was unable to lift me on his own, so he called his older brother for assistance. While we waited for his brother to arrive, I apologized to my husband for the situation, and we both began to cry as we sat on the floor. In that moment, my husband reassured me, saying, "I've got you."

During my healing process, my husband worked two jobs. He would come home from one and prepare me for the day; helping me shower, get dressed, and preparing my meals before leaving for his second job. The church and I prayed for God to strengthen him throughout this process.

My brother-in-law eventually arrived at the house. Together, they helped me up off of the floor. He then told my husband that I needed a wheelchair; however, after he left, I informed my husband that I did not need one.

That same day my husband had to call 911 to request an ambulance so they could help lift me and take me to the hospital. I did not want to go back to Houston Medical Center… I wanted a second opinion; so, the paramedics took me to Atrium Health Navicent in Peach County.

While in the back of the ambulance, the Lord spoke to me and said, "You do not have Multiple Sclerosis."

The attending doctor at Atrium Health Navicent requested my records from Houston Medical Center.
I didn't have any records with me, so they contacted Houston Medical Center

directly. They also ran additional tests; after which, the doctor stated that I had Multiple Sclerosis.

After the doctor left my ER cubicle, I shared with my husband what the Lord had spoken to me in the back of the ambulance. I chose to believe the report of the Lord!

"Who hath believed our report? And to whom is the arm of the Lord revealed?"

Isaiah 53:1 (KJV)

"Forever, O Lord, Your word is settled in heaven (standing firm and unchangeable)."

Psalm 119:89 (AMP)

In my heart and mind, I was determined to stand firmly and cling to what God said. Nothing and no one was going to move me from that belief. I trusted in, relied upon, and held on to every word God spoke. He said that I was healed and that I did not have that autoimmune disease. I refused to grow weary or doubt. God said it, and I believed just that.

The ER nurse told me I needed to get a cane so that I wouldn't keep falling down. She shared that it would help support my balance. She then went on to explain how to walk with the cane in my right hand so it could support my left side. When we left, we went to Walmart to purchase a cane. Once again, I expressed to my husband that I was going to beat and overcome it because I did not have MS.

One night, I fell again. This time while trying to get back in bed after getting up to use the restroom. At that time, my youngest daughter was home. She tried to help me up but was unable to, so she called 911 and the paramedics came lifted me up off of the floor.

One of the paramedics asked what was going on with me. I told him the hospital had diagnosed me with MS but that I did not have it. One of the same paramedics who had previously taken me to the hospital in Byron walked in, called me by name then mentioned my diagnosis to his coworker.

The first paramedic asked, “Are you sure she has MS? It doesn’t look like she has it.” The second paramedic replied that I had just been diagnosed and that it can come on aggressively. Once again, I emphasized to them that I did not have MS and that I was going to overcome what I was dealing with. I politely requested that they place me in my recliner because I didn't want to scare my daughter again. That day I decided not to resume sleeping in my bed until I became strong enough to lift my left side onto the bed without assistance.

I kept repeating, "I believe the report of the Lord," because that Word had to be firmly established in my heart and mind for my healing to come to pass. I walked with the cane for two to three weeks, then I heard the Lord say, "Walk in My strength."

John 5:8 reads, **"Jesus saith unto him, Rise, take up thy bed, and walk."**

"But the salvation of the righteous is of the Lord: He is their strength in the time of trouble. And the Lord shall help them, and deliver them: He shall deliver them from the wicked, and save them, because they trust in Him."

Psalm 37:39-40 (KJV)

"Fear thou not; for I am with thee: be not dismayed; for I am thy God: I will strengthen thee; yea, I will help thee yea, I will uphold thee with the right hand of my righteousness"

Isaiah 41:10 (KJV)

I placed the cane in my closet and told my family from then on, I would walk in God's strength. I began walking slowly...but I was walking in God's strength. My husband would often keep the cane near me or tell me to get it but instead of using it I would hold it up in the air with my right hand. I was determined to rely on God's strength and not my own.

2 Corinthians 1:8-11 (MSG) says, **"...instead of trusting in our own strength or wits to get out of it, we were forced to trust God totally – not a bad idea since He's the God who raises the dead!"**

When I went out in public people often stared, asked if I was okay, or questioned where my cane was, I always responded by saying, "I'm okay. God is my cane (staff)," or I would simply say, "I am walking in God's strength."

"Yea, though I walk through the valley of the shadow of death, I will fear no

evil: for Thou art with me; Thy rod and Thy staff, they comfort me"

Psalm 23:4 (KJV)

I could not do it without God. I am not my own. I belong to Him.

One Sunday, my Pastor came by to see how I was doing and to pray over me. After examining my arm, she told my husband and I that it was weak and that I needed to see a physical therapist as soon as possible.

I began searching for physical therapists in my area and came across Pinnacle Physical Therapy & Sports Medicine. I read through the reviews and found many great success stories of people recovering in a short period of time. I called to ask whether I needed a doctor's referral or if I could begin right away. The receptionist informed me that a referral was not required, so I scheduled an appointment for an evaluation.

In the meantime, while waiting for my appointment in Atlanta, I struggled with brain fog that made it challenging for me to focus and concentrate on reading God's Word. I felt intense pressure in both my head and eyes. However, I refused to dwell on the pain. Instead, I would say, "I am going through my healing process," or, "I am having a healing moment."

I played the Bible app on my phone while I slept because I did not want any negativity to enter my mind. My husband often prayed for me, and both quoted and read scriptures over me. He constantly spoke life into me, saying, "I see you getting stronger," or simply, "You are strong." He told me this every single day.

When I was able to focus, I read Ezekiel 37:1-14 and Matthew 12:13, and I prayed those Scriptures over myself daily. My husband also exercised my arm each day, lifting it, moving it back and forth, while praying over it as he did.

One evening, the Lord spoke to me and said, "Anoint your arm and prophesy." I anointed my arm with the oil I had received from my Bishop, Daniel Akins, and I prophesied Ezekiel 37:1-14 over it. The very next day, I was able to move my arm a little. I began praising God and asked my husband to record me moving it. I wanted to document the evidence of the Holy Spirit at work.

The following day, the Atlanta Neuroscience Institute called to schedule my appointment with a neurologist. The appointment was set a few days before my physical therapy evaluation.

When I went to see the neurologist in Atlanta, she conducted her own evaluation. She asked me several questions about what I was feeling and the symptoms I was experiencing. I told her I was dealing with brain fog, fatigue, loss of balance, muscle cramping, urinary incontinence, inflammation, and slurred speech.

I explained that I believed much of what I was experiencing was due to inflammation in my body. The doctor questioned, "How do you know it's just inflammation?" I replied that my skin and joints felt inflamed.

She did not respond right away. Instead, she asked if I had undergone steroid therapy. I told her yes, but it had not worked. She seemed surprised that the treatment was unsuccessful. She then asked why I was wearing a sling on my arm. I explained that my arm had given out while I was exercising, and I had been unable to move it for an entire month. She stated that MS does not typically cause an arm to "go out" like that. She suggested it might be a pinched nerve and scheduled an MRI to determine whether there was a nerve issue in my neck.

She also arranged physical therapy for my left arm at Pinnacle Physical Therapy & Sports Medicine. I was excited to hear that it wasn't anything serious affecting my arm.

After reviewing my CT scan and MRI, the neurologist informed me that there were lesions on my brain. She discussed several medication options that could help me recover more quickly and return to my normal life. However, I told her that I did not want to take medication. Instead, I asked about following a nutritional plan.

She explained that she was not a nutritionist but provided pamphlets with information about the Mediterranean diet, various medications, and the different stages of MS for me to review. Then she instructed me to call her office within a week to let her know which medication I had decided to take.

When I arrived home, I looked through the medication pamphlets and asked God, "Which medicine do You want me to take?" I heard the Holy Spirit say, "I am your medicine." My husband was in the next room, and I immediately told him what the Lord had said. I then called and texted the leaders of my church and my family to share what God had spoken. I told them, "I'm going to walk this out."

The following day, I returned to Atlanta for an MRI of my neck to determine whether I had a pinched nerve. However, the results showed I did not have a pinched nerve. A week passed, and I had not called the doctor to choose a medication. Instead, I began researching the Mediterranean diet.

The Mediterranean diet focuses on eating fruits, vegetables, nuts, whole grains, legumes, and olive oil, while incorporating moderate amounts of dairy, poultry, eggs, and fish. The Lord impressed upon me the importance of eating more greens. He reminded me of Revelation 22:2, which says, **"The leaves of the tree were for the healing of the nations."** I also noticed in the pamphlet that patients with MS were encouraged to eat more vegetables and fruits than anything else.

I decided to follow the Mediterranean diet and in obedience to God's Word, I began increasing my intake of grains, fruits, and vegetables. The Lord instructed me to remain on this diet and not to return to my previous eating habits.

The next day, I began physical therapy. My therapist and his team created a plan to address my neuropathy symptoms. Part of the treatment included using a machine similar to a TENS unit, designed to stimulate and awaken the nerves in the body.

In addition to the treatments, I also did exercises to strengthen my muscles, improve my nerves, and help with my coordination. These included opening clothespins with my left hand, using a pulley to stretch and move my left arm, working my quadriceps, and other strengthening exercises.

Two weeks later, it was time for my follow-up appointment at the Atlanta Neuroscience Institute. When we arrived, my husband and I sat in the examination room waiting to be seen. When the doctor finally came in, the first thing she asked was, "Which medication did you decide to take?"

I informed her that I had decided not to take any medication. She responded by asking, "Then why are you here?" I explained that I was there for my scheduled follow-up appointment. I also told her that I had prayed about the medication and that the Lord had instructed me not to take it.

She looked at my shirt…I was wearing a Christian shirt with an image of Jesus Christ on it. She gave a slight smirk and glanced at my husband, but he didn't say anything. She then began asking questions such as, "Are you having headaches?" It felt as though she was trying to determine whether I was being delusional.

I calmly told her that I could clearly hear and that I knew the voice of my God. She continued asking questions while explaining the risk factors of the disease; seemingly trying to frighten me into changing my mind. I politely told her, "You cannot force me to take medication."

She replied, "Well, it's your body." I responded, "No, it's God's body."

She then asked if she could continue to monitor my condition, and I agreed. Before leaving the room, she handed me a paper listing several medications and told me to think about it. After she left, the Holy Spirit told me to throw the paper in the trash, and I did.

While my husband was driving us home, I heard the Holy Spirit say, "You are radical." Meaning that I have radical faith. When we arrived home, the Spirit of the Lord spoke again and said, "Fast."

The Lord led me to pray three times a day: morning, noon, and evening; just as Daniel did. This, I understood, was God's medicine.

We take man-made medication on a similar set schedule: morning, noon, and evening. If we would only turn to God, He will direct our paths when it comes to our individual healing processes.

During my times of prayer, I cried out to the Lord, asking for forgiveness and for the healing of my body,
However, I continued attending physical

therapy to help stimulate my nerves, strengthen my muscles, and improve my coordination. After about a month, the Lord instructed me not to allow the therapist to place me back on the machine that stimulated my nerves. The physical therapist was shocked but happy to see that I was walking by faith and boldly claiming my healing.

The physical therapist instructed me to drive around my neighborhood to help improve coordination on the left side of my body. At first, I could only turn right. It was a challenge for me to turn left, but as I continued exercising my left arm, I gradually gained the ability to use it to turn left just a little. I was in a lot of pain, but I kept pushing and praying.

One day the Lord said, “It’s time for you to walk it out.” Even so, I stayed in therapy for another month so that I could learn the exercises well enough to continue them at home. When my last day arrived, I told the physical therapist that I would not be returning for any more sessions; It was time for me to walk it out with God’s guidance.

When I returned home, I went into my prayer closet and cried out to God for healing in my body. After praying, I began researching ways to improve brain health. During my search, I came across a video by Barbara O’Neill explaining that the body can grow new brain nerves between the hours of 8:00 p.m. and 5:00 a.m. while a person is sleeping. Studies have shown that sleep plays an important role in maintaining the health of nerve cells, called neurons, and can even contribute to the growth of new neurons in the brain.

One night, my mind was restless and I couldn't sleep because of the discomfort I was feeling in my head. The Holy Spirit spoke to me and said, "Be still." So, I prayed that my body and my mind would be still in Jesus' name. A calmness came over me, and the mind racing and pain I was experiencing subsided.

I was finally able to rest and get some sound sleep. I had to stop fighting in my mind and trust that God is superior over every situation. It reminded me of when Jesus was sleeping in the boat during a storm while the waves crashed against it. He rebuked the storm and there was a calmness on the sea. As it says in Mark 4:39 (GNT), **"Jesus stood up and**

commanded the wind, 'Be quiet!" and He said to the waves, 'Be still!' The wind died down, and there was a great calm."

I began playing the Bible app on my phone while I slept so that the Word of God would remain in my spirit. I did not want to give the enemy any room to enter, while I slept, during my healing process. When you are in right standing with God, you can truly rest because God has you, and nothing can come near your dwelling. Because of His protection, you are able to withstand every attack.

LET THE HEALING BEGIN

When God first told me to fast, I did not do it fully. I would only fast for a couple of days here and there. However, the Lord instructed me to fast again.

Fasting plays an important role in the healing process. The best way to fast is to abstain from food, and when prayer is added to fasting, it draws you closer to God. Jesus is the Bread of Life. When you consume God's Word while fasting, His Word fills you and the Holy Spirit who resides in you, pulls you closer to God. He removes anything that causes disconnection from God.

Yes, we need food to nourish our bodies (temples), but when we overeat, it creates a disconnect from the presence of God.

You must make room for Him within you because He desires to dwell there. Overeating can lead to various ailments and sluggishness, and it can hinder the Spirit of God. The Lord says, "Make room for Me." This is why we turn down our plates and enter into the presence of God.

Fasting also helps remove toxins from the body and supports the repair of cells. It becomes part of the journey of rebuilding the temple (body), while also restoring a closer relationship with God.

In the Bible, we see examples of rebuilding the temple; such as in the book of Ezra. The Israelites were in captivity in Babylon, but God stirred the spirit of King Cyrus to make a proclamation to rebuild the temple (the house of the Lord), which had been destroyed by the Babylonians.

In many ways, my body had been in captivity because of my own sinful patterns; pleasing my flesh and moving in disobedience instead of honoring God's temple. I wasn't out there committing adultery or living recklessly in the streets; however, I was not obeying God's instructions for my life, and I had drawn away from Him.

At first, I did not fully recognize it. But as I began rebuilding my relationship with God, I realized what had happened. I had served God all my life, yet disobedience can still cause a person to be in captivity. The Bible clearly teaches that we should not separate ourselves, disconnect, or draw back from God.

When we separate ourselves from God, we become vulnerable to spiritual attacks.

In Matthew 8:28, there is a story about two men who were possessed by demons. When they came into the presence of the Lord, the men were set free. However, the unclean spirits asked Jesus for permission to enter a herd of pigs that were a distance away. Jesus gave them permission, and the spirits entered the pigs.

I realized that because I had drawn back and was not in God's presence as I should have been, I had made myself vulnerable, and an unclean spirit had attacked my body. I had to build an altar and restore my temple. There was no way around it. I was in ruins because my flesh was still alive. My flesh had to die.

I began praying three times a day to rebuild my relationship with my Heavenly

Father. I cried out to God for healing, and during that process, I repented before the Lord for days, asking Him to show me where I had sinned, and He revealed those areas to me.

Repentance means a change of mind. It involves turning away from the wrong one has done and making a sincere decision to change for the better. True repentance comes with an abhorrence of one's past sins. If I wanted God to heal my body, I needed to restore my relationship with my Heavenly Father through repentance and asking for forgiveness.

I had to lay myself on the altar as a living sacrifice, setting myself apart so that God could take hold of me. I had to give Him all of me; full control over my life.

During one of my intimate moments with the Lord, the Holy Spirit spoke to me and said, "I am going to realign, refine, and reform you."

Realignment is the act of changing or restoring something to a different or former position or state. **Refining** is the act of removing impurities or unwanted substance. It is also means to improve something by making specific changes, and is a more subtle and accurate process of separating. The word **reform** means to make changes to improve something. This process often involves correcting false, abusive, or unsatisfactory conditions within a system, institution, or practice.

God began realigning, refining, and reforming me through His Word. He also gave me an exercise routine and a meal plan to help transform both my mind and my body so that my life would align with His Will.

When you continually remain in God's presence and fully surrender to Him, He will guide you in every area of your life. God had to take me through a purification process, shaping me into another vessel.

I realized that I had been doing things according to the world's way of thinking instead of fully trusting God in every area of my life. Psalm 37:5 (KJV), tells us to: **"Commit all our ways to the Lord, trust also in Him, and He will bring it to pass."** I had only been giving Him part of my life; not all of it.

God wants every part of us, our thoughts, our careers, our schedules, our children, our vacation plans...even our meal plans and how we dress. This is what God wants. We cannot do this halfway. We cannot serve worldly values more than we serve God. I could not serve two masters. Yes, I was in church serving the Lord, praying and fasting, on the praise team, and in leadership, but I was only giving Him half of me; not all of me. I wasn't the "living sacrifice" he wanted me to be.

A living sacrifice means offering your entire life to God's service. That includes your mind, body, and soul. It is an ongoing process of totally surrendering to God so that He can continue to transform you.

We tend to go back to our old ways of living, in what we eat, the careers we pursue, how we dress, the makeup we wear, the cars we choose to buy, the areas we decide to live in, etc. When we do not fully surrender ourselves to God, we are bowing to lesser gods and following the ways of the world rather than God's way.

God had to strip me and purify me. He had to destroy, pluck up, and tear down the things in my flesh that were ruining me because I was not fully walking in the righteousness of Jesus Christ.

The doctor informed me that I could not be under stress because it triggered my immune system to attack my nerves; essentially causing my body to attack itself. During my quiet time with the Lord, I told Him that I did not feel stressed. So, I began to examine the different events and responsibilities in my life, my business, family, ministry, and even my exercise routines, to see what may have been causing me to become stressed.

As I reflected on these areas, the Lord began to shine His light on them. I realized that I had been trying to manage ministry, family, and business on my own instead of giving those responsibilities to God and allowing Him to help me manage them.

I also had a deeper conversation with the Lord about the food I was eating, especially since He had instructed me to follow the Mediterranean diet. I asked God if the food I had been consuming could be contributing to the stress in my body. Through that process, I discovered that certain foods were indeed causing stress within my body.

I had been experiencing mood swings and ungodly thoughts. My emotions were unbalanced, and my hormones were out of control. All of this was affecting my walk with Christ. God revealed that **I only needed to eat from His table**. I had to choose to eat life, not death.

I began to realize that I had been all over the place, trying to handle everything in my own strength. During my purification process, God began to purge me as I broke up the fallow ground of my heart by diligently seeking Him through His Word, fasting, and prayer.

The enemy had me imprisoned in my own body through this condition, where my body was attacking itself. As God began to reveal things to me, He showed me that certain foods were causing inflammation in my body; especially processed foods and seasonings that had been created in laboratories. When I understood this, I removed all of my seasonings and threw them out. I replaced them with natural spices and herbs that God created; things that would bring life and nourishment to my body; which is God's temple.

God was stripping away my old garments (my old ways of thinking, my habits, and my former way of eating), and clothing me with new garments. Processed foods often appeal strongly to the flesh, causing us to crave more of them. This craving is a form of lust.

For example, many believers in the body of Christ may fast from sugar, fast food, or other things that please the flesh. However, once the fast is over, they often return to those same habits. In my case, it was my old way of eating. Sometimes we even find ourselves eating more than we did before the fast.

When fasting, we often look to God to change our mindset, behavior, and habits. Yet we rarely consider the food that the world places in front of us and how it is affecting God's temple (our bodies).

God used fasting and prayer to purify me both spiritually and physically. It humbled me, drew me deeper into the Word of God, and helped me focus on God's promises for my life so that my mind could be renewed and aligned with His Word.

Spiritually, fasting helped remove distractions, negative thoughts, unhealthy desires, and traditions that were defiling my spirit. **Naturally,** the fasting God chose for me helped remove damaged cells from my body through the body's elimination process. Fasting triggers a cellular rebooting phase known as autophagy, which helps the body clean out and repair itself.

According to research, the body is able to recycle old, damaged, or weak cells and components in order to conserve energy and generate new, healthy cells. During this process, all the toxins that were stored in my cells began to be released from my body.

Jesus is the Living Cornerstone. He is strong, unchanging, and unbreakable. He is the sure foundation of my life. Through prayer, I was becoming like a living stone, gaining stability in my life through prayer and fasting.

Yes, there were times when I wobbled while walking or when I bent down, but as I surrendered myself fully to God and His Word, He began to strengthen my body, soul, and mind. I became anchored in God's Word, and nothing could move me from that foundation. His Word is a firm foundation.

As Psalm 40:2 says, **"He brought me up out of a horrible pit, out of the miry**

clay, and set my feet upon a rock, and established my steps."

When God told me He was going to strengthen my core, I began to declare that my body would become like God's temple; refined and purified like gold. God did just what He said He would do. He instructed me on how to eat His seed; which is life. Jesus is the Living Bread, the Living Cornerstone, and the Living Seed!

While fasting, I spent more time in repentance each day during my time of prayer before the Lord. I continually asked God to show me where I had sinned. The Lord revealed an area in my life where I had been disobedient. He had called me to take a leadership position in ministry. Although I accepted the position, I was not operating in the fullness of my calling as a leader.

This reminded me of a dream God had given me years earlier. In the dream, the Lord warned me that if I did not accept and walk in this calling, I would end up on a bed of affliction. Even though I had taken the position, I was not fully walking it out. That was still disobedience, and I realized that I was sinning against God.

When I understood this, I cried even harder before the Lord, asking Him to forgive me. In that moment, it felt as if prison doors had opened and I heard the Lord say, "***You are free from your captivity.***" As I cried out in prayer, I heard what sounded like a demon screaming. My crying soon turned into praise. The enemy thought he had me, but God snatched me out of his hands.

It was in that place of deep crying, repentance, and persistent pressing that I began to understand how spiritual stamina is developed. It is not formed in comfort, but in surrender. It is built in the moments when you refuse to stop praying, when your flesh is tired, your voice is weak, and your heart is heavy, yet you continue to press into God.

I told the Lord that I would walk in this calling in its fullness. I also told my family not to make the same mistake I had made. If God calls you to do anything for His Kingdom, do it.

The Lord also warned me that if I were to draw back again, I would continue to fall and would lose sight in my left eye. That was not God's desire for me; it was a warning about the enemy's plan.

Matthew 12:43-45 says, **"When an unclean spirit is gone out of a man, he walketh through dry places, seeking rest, and findeth none. Then he saith, I will return into my house from whence I came out; and when he is come, findeth it empty, swept and garnished. Then goeth he, and taketh with himself seven other spirits more wicked than**

himself, and they enter in and dwell there: and the last state of that man is worse than the first."

That passage truly woke me up! I understood that God was warning me and that realization shined a light on my life. I asked God to help me walk in this calling. I thought my fasting was over, but the God said, "No, go back into fasting and praying." He was taking me into a deeper stage of refining and reforming.

Through this testing and the affliction in my body, God was removing impurities from both my body and my spirit that were not of Him. He was separating me from the world's ways of unrighteousness and teaching me to walk fully in His righteousness. I realized that I had not been fully obeying God. My disobedience was sin, and that is not the character of Jesus Christ.

God had to get me and my flesh out of the way so that I could truly live in righteousness. My thought patterns had been out of alignment with the Word of God, especially emotionally. I was often moody, and many things irritated my spirit and I did not have inner peace within myself.

On the outside, I walked around every day as if I had peace but at the end of the day, inwardly I did not. At times, I would take that frustration out on my family or even within the church through my actions. Not in an evil way, but I carried a harshness and an attitude of greater authority that said, "you're not going to move me" which made it difficult for me to yield or submit in some areas.

REBIRTH

The Holy Spirit washed me and made me whole again. I was dead in my grave of disobedience but the Lord raised me up so that I could follow Him. As John 8:36 (KJV) says, **"If the Son therefore shall make you free, ye shall be free indeed."**

Before anyone can fully receive the Kingdom of God, there must first be a rebirth. Jesus explained this in John 3:3 (KJV): **"Verily, verily, I say unto thee, except a man be born again, he cannot see the kingdom of God."**

The Lord came and searched my heart, revealing to me just how powerful He truly is. I've come to realize that every person has a cup designed specifically for them; a cup that no one else can carry.

God wants us to continually come into His presence so that He can continually refill our cup.

I wanted more of God because I desired to be healed by Him, physically, spiritually, and in my daily walk with Him. I did not want to continue living in disobedience. God is showing me the difference in my walk with Him and I thank Him for the transformation that has made me whole again; because I no longer wanted to live in disobedience.

God began teaching me how to carry His mercy and His grace in my life by remaining in His presence.

God desires for you to shine in His presence. Even through our afflictions and in the latter seasons of our lives, He has called us to be different and wants us to remain faithful to Him and reflect His light until the very end.

I continued to ask God to remove every dead thing from my life so that I can live the life He wants me to live before Him. I asked Him to remove every idol and anything lifeless within me so that I could once again live fully in His presence.

God's hands have been gracious toward me!

THE SPIRIT OF GLUTTONY

The spirit of gluttony reveals a lack of discipline when it comes to both God's spiritual nourishment and the natural food He provides. During this journey, I began following the Mediterranean diet. As I continued, God showed me that meat was not agreeing with my body. I eventually reduced my meat intake to once a day, eating only salmon.

During prayer, I began asking God, "Where did this desire for meat come from?" He led me to the Book of Genesis. I realized that Adam spent time in the presence of the Lord, but Eve did not have the same encounter with God. When Adam listened to Eve and ate the forbidden fruit, his eyes were opened, and he realized they were naked.

Through these scriptures, God showed me that when humanity fell in the flesh, people began to crave the flesh (meat). That's where it began. I told the Lord; I didn't want it. I didn't want to be reminded of man's sin. I asked Him to remove my desire for meat (flesh) and He did.

I also prayed, "Lord, you've blessed me with two daughters. Please deliver me from Eve's sin as well." And He did…God delivered me from Eve's sin. I did not want to be reminded of Adam's sin nor Eve's. . . it was already enough that I had to remember my own.

Through this healing process, God developed a new discipline within me, both in the Word of God and in the way I ate the natural foods He provided. I had to experience a spiritual dying of the old self because my soul had been dying while I was feeding it junk from the world's system. That "junk food" had no life in it for my soul. I was constantly on a temporary "sugar high," while my spirit was starving.

In the book of Daniel, we see how Daniel remained connected to God. In a similar way, the Lord led my family and me to focus on seed-bearing foods that carry life. Foods without seed carry death. Seeds represent life and growth. Jesus Himself is the Living Bread of Life, and He is also the seed that carries life within Him; a seed that spreads life among His people.

Daniel refused to defile himself by eating the king's food because it represented the world's system. He did not want to lose his identity or his connection with God. Instead, he wanted pulse (Jesus' heartbeat; seeds of the Kingdom). In the same way, I refused to allow a diagnosis to define my identity. I was not going to accept the label that the doctors placed on me because I belong to the Kingdom of God.

Today's processed food carries no life in it and it causes a lot harm our bodies, because it is dead, not alive.

FEARLESS

"God is our refuge and strength, a very present help in trouble.

Psalm 46:1

(KJV) Being fearless does not mean there is an absence of challenges; but rather the presence of a promise. To walk without fear, I first had to recognize that my strength is not self-generated; it does not come from myself. My strength is found in the refuge of my Heavenly Father.

THE STRATEGY OF BATTLE READINESS

For me to be ready for the giant that stood in my way, I had to adopt a spiritual battle formation. This is not a physical position but a position of the heart and mind.

- **Internalize the Truth (Psalm 119:11 KJV): "Thy word have I hid in mine heart, that I might not sin against thee"**

The Word of God is our ammunition. When it is hidden in our heart, it becomes an instinctive shield against fear.

- **Stay the Course (Joshua 1:7 KJV): Be strong and very courageous. Do not turn to the right or the left.**

Others may offer you their armor, their opinions, their methods, or their fears, but I had to remember that God has equipped me uniquely. Use the armor God gave you to battle with.

- **Constant Meditation (Joshua 1:8 KJV): Let the Word never depart**

from your mouth. Meditate on it day and night.

This is your Jordan; the place of laying prostrate in prayer and fasting. It is in this place of surrender that you will find your greatest power.

Don't be intimidated by challenges that arise in the morning or in the evening. . . you can overcome them. Move into battle formation, shout with a war cry, move into position and face the challenge(s) in battle formation. Get in the presence of the Lord and read His Words; He will give you grace and a strategy just like He gave David grace to bring Goliath down with five stones.

God has graced me with scriptures to come against every challenge that wants to stand tall in my life. Every giant shall fall and every challenge shall fall. This is how you become fearless.

FAITH

I'm standing on Gods promises for my life. He told me that I would be healed and that I had to trust and believe Him. I left everything that was familiar to me and my family behind to walk this journey out; stepping out in faith demands that you grab a hold of a promise without evening knowing what's ahead. I have seen miracles in my family while growing up. I saw my father be healed from diabetes before the Lord called Him home. He was always on his knees every morning praying to God. I took hold of that. If God could do it for my father, He could do it for me. Just like Abram, his wife Sarah took a hold of his faith to trust and believe God's plan for her to conceive even though she was barren and past childbearing age. They showed us that we are living in a different Kingdom not this world's kingdom. We live in heavenly realms. This is why God wants our hearts to be fixed on Him, so we won't go back to our familiar places.

God's word is alive. The Lord said that if you have living faith the size of a mustard seed, you can move mountains. However, some things can only be moved through prayer and fasting. You must have faith while fasting and praying, choosing to trust God to move in that specific are of your life. Your faith grows when you water it with prayer and feed it with fasting and the Word of God.
"And Jesus said unto them, because of your unbelief: for verily I say unto you, if ye have faith as a grain of mustard seed, ye shall say unto this mountain,

remove hence to yonder place; and it shall remove; and nothing shall be impossible unto you."

Matthew 17:20 (KJV)

One day after praying, I laid back down in bed and felt God's hand straightening my spine. The next day, I was standing much taller than I had been before. It reminded me of Isaiah 40:4 which says, **"Every valley shall be exalted, and every mountain and hill shall be made low: and the crooked shall be made straight, and the rough places plain" (KJV).**

In that moment, I felt as though God was not only straightening my body but also re-aligning my life.

Romans 8:4 says, **"So now every righteous requirement of the law can be fulfilled through the Anointed One living his life in us. And we are free to live, not according to our flesh, but by the dynamic power of the Holy Spirit" (TPT).**

One Sunday during service, while all of this was still unfolding in my life, I was sitting on the front row at church while prayer was taking place. I bowed my head and prayed quietly to God, saying I only wanted to walk in His Spirit at all times. In that moment, I heard the Lord say, ***"It is granted unto you."***

I no longer wanted to be led by my flesh. I wanted to be led by the Spirit of God. That was when God empowered me with His Holy Spirit. As the scriptures says, the

Holy Spirit lives in us. I surrendered myself to the Lord so that His Spirit could dwell within me.

TOTAL SURRENDER TO GOD

I gave myself completely to God while in my prayer closet; dwelling in His presence. When God desires all of you, you cannot give Him only a part of yourself. I could no longer offer Him just a part of me. The Word tells us to, **"present ourselves as a living sacrifice, holy and acceptable to God" (Romans 12:1 KJV).**

I had to re-dedicate every area of my life to God, including my thoughts, my concerns, the food I ate, how I dressed, my affliction. . .everything. When you lay yourself before God, you cannot leave anything out.

God says in Matthew 11:28, "**Come to me, all who are weary and burdened, and I will give you rest" (KJV).**

When you truly follow God and you allow the Holy Spirit to lead you, He refreshes you and your life becomes joined with His life, because you recognize that you can do nothing without Him.

When you fully surrender to God, you begin to bear the fruit of the Spirit: inner peace, kindness, gentleness, joy, love, long-suffering, goodness, faith, meekness, and temperance (self-control).

In Luke 9:23, Jesus told His followers, "**If you truly desire to be my disciple, you must disown your life completely, embrace my cross and your own and surrender to my ways" (KJV).**

I told God, "You can take it all from me because I belong to You." When I did that, I felt freedom in my spirit. Recently, when

I was baptized, the covenant was sealed and stamped with approval. I am not my own anymore. I belong to Jesus Christ.

I am no longer conformed to the values of this world. Instead of relying on my own understanding, I chose to trust in the Lord with all my heart. When I did, God began directing every step of my healing journey.

He gave me the exercises and the meal plan. He also instructed me on what kind of exercises to do from walking, rebounding, and stretching my limbs. Eventually, He led me to a plant-based lifestyle. Every instruction was for my body and for my obedience, because my deepest desire was to remain connected to Him.

Now, I am at peace with God. I have become like a fortified city; secure in the salvation I've found through Jesus Christ. My mind is fixed on Him, and He has made me whole because I remained consistent in seeking God's Kingdom and His righteousness.

When I stood at the crossroads between what the doctors prescribed and what God had spoken, I made a decision that would define the rest of my journey.

The world offered me a cane, steroids, and a lifelong diagnosis; but heaven offered me healing.

I chose to believe the voice of God.

The reports told what my body was experiencing, but that could not override what my Creator had declared. When the

Holy Spirit said, "I am your medicine," it was not just comfort it was instruction.

In that moment, I understood: God was calling me to trust Him beyond fear, beyond symptoms, and beyond the limitations of human understanding.

This journey was never just about a physical condition. It was about surrender. It was about faith.
It was about choosing the King's table over everything the world offered me.

The world has its medicine...and it has its place. But I came to know a Healer who is greater than any diagnosis, more powerful than any prescription, and more faithful than any report. What man calls impossible, God has already done.
I made up my mind to walk this out; not

in denial, but in faith. Not in fear, but in authority. Not leaning on what I could see but standing on what God had spoken.

". . . It is written, Man shall not live by bread alone, but by every word that proceedeth out of the mouth of God"

Matt. 4:4 (KJV)

And as I walked, He met me. He healed me. He restored me both spiritually and physically. . .just as He promised.

This is my testimony. God is still the Balm of Gilead. He is still the Great Physician and He is still able to do exceedingly, abundantly above all we could ever ask or think. So, I leave you with this truth:

No matter the report you've been given, no matter what your body is saying, and regardless of what the world has prescribed, there is a seat prepared for you at **The King's Table**, and at His table, there is healing.